The Poems of Lucy Snowe

A.B. FLYNN

FEROS FERIO PRESS

Contents

For Jared.

—A.B. Flynn

Preface

I don't remember writing my first poem, but considering that I was writing and recording "songs" (on a cassette tape, of course) by the time I was six years old, I can assume it happened as soon as I could grasp what a rhyme was. My childhood was full of poetry—nursery rhymes, songs, and Biblical prose. By the time I was ten, I was coaxing poems out of my younger siblings line by line in an attempt to educate them on the process.

The first poem of note I remember was *The Lady of Shallot* by Alfred, Lord Tennyson (due to its prominence in the 1987 adaptation of *Anne of Green Gables*, starring Megan Follows), and it became the golden fleece of poetry to me. If I could write words like that, I thought, I would be a real poet.

What followed were years of cheesy, cliché-riddled attempts to capture the chivalry and romance that danced in my head, and in my mid-teens, I gave it up to focus on my fiction writing. I was not a poet, I decided—and that was alright. I would write books instead.

A decade later, I dipped my toes into poetry once more, allowing myself the freedom of ignoring rhyme and rules, and letting magical words flow as they would. That was the birth of this collection, written from 2014 to 2019—some of the most notable and formative years of my life. That period was filled with emotional hardship and pain, but from the suffering came a newfound creativity. The agony in my heart was so great that it forced my hand. Poetry seemed the only release: a way to capture the suffering and find something beautiful.

During those years, I experienced professional success, moments of bliss, an abusive relationship, a broken heart, the loss of my religious faith, and the untimely death of a childhood friend. The poems that capture these events are all in this collection. The title is drawn from the heroine of Charlotte Brontë's *Villette*—a pseudonym I considered using when I had so much pain and shame connected to my life experiences that I was determined to publish the collection anonymously. Now, being on the other side of that darkness, I want to honor that painful time while still giving these words my name.

Thus, *The Poems of Lucy Snowe*. I hope you find a piece of yourself here.

—A.B. Flynn

The flash of passion was all over very soon. He smiled as he told me to wipe my eyes; he waited quietly till I was calm, dropping from time to time a stilling, solacing word. Ere long I sat beside him once more myself—re-assured, not desperate, nor yet desolate; not friendless, not hopeless, not sick of life, and seeking death.

"It made you very sad then to lose your friend?" said he.

"It kills me to be forgotten, Monsieur," I said.

—Charlotte Brontë, *Vilette*

THE MOON LAUGHS

It's high in the sky, catching my eye, as I step outside, the ground hard beneath me, my breath like smoke, cold around me.

It's all a glisten, paper thin, a Cheshire grin, looking down at me, peering, prying, trying to know.

I shiver, quiver, as I eye the sliver, it's a sinister smile, and I can't escape it, no matter where I go.

I stare, aware, my breath hot in the icy air, waiting like a cat to spring, to run, always on guard, apprehensive.

What does the night sky want from me? What have I done?

I ask the moon. The moon laughs.

January 2014

MEMORIES OF THE DRAGON

I walk alone, holding hands with the ghost of what has been.
The bridge beneath my feet is missing rungs.
I can't look, or I might plummet.
But if I fall, a winged dragon will catch me.
I'll fly away
And the daylight will kiss my eyelids
And the moonlight will fade into the lakes below
Where I watch my shadows, dancing gaily
Like mermaids beneath the surface of the sea:
Playful companions, gesturing.

They want me to join them
But if I lose my breath, it will not return
And if I use my wishes, the genie will be gone.
I'll find myself imprisoned in a palace
With stones in my pockets where coins used to be
And my arms wrapped around the skeleton of a lover
Who left me his body and took his soul away to paradise.

There is a skylight above, painting flowers that skip across the sun
But I don't want to take part in such happiness.
I'd rather languish, and let the tears run
And the laughter echo
And the memories of the dragon drive me sane
Until sleep at last has found me.

November 2014

AN OLD POEM ON A NEW DAY OF SNOW

The snow fell while I slept
Caressed the pane
Cried my name
With tiny flakes of winter's flame
And through the fissures crept.

The snow fell while I slept
And yet unseen
It met each dream
And painted it a frosty scene
As down the blizzard swept.

The snow fell while I slept
The world bathed white
Through all the night
And blinded eyes by morning light
In wafting, wondrous depth.

December 2014

NEVER

I'm in love with a ghost.

The ghost of a past I never knew and a summer we never spent
together.

When we never held each other tight in the tall grass
        and watched the clouds above our heads.
When you never kissed my lips until they bled
        and held my hand until our fingers caught flame.
When the wind never whipped my hair out the window of your
Chevrolet,
        and the sun never burned the skin upon my bare shoulders.

When your eyes never smiled,
        and your laughter never filled the four walls of my bedroom.

And my heart never beat faster than yours.

And I never lived.
And I never loved.
And the ghosts never haunted me.

April 2015

ALICE AND AMANDA'S POEM

Life, what is it but a dream?
Things are never what they seem:
Masquerading moonlight schemes.

Dreaming as the summers die,
Straining for the heron's cry,
Echoing the endless, "why?"

Lovingly shall nestle near
Each evasive leeching fear
Roaming round this earthly sphere.

Never seen by waking eyes
Is the maiden fair with lies,
Turned away with every tide.

Autumn frosts have slain July.
Springtime hearts that should not sigh
Walk into the wintertime.

Pleased a simple tale to hear,
Loath to drop a burden dear,
The tired, twisted whisperer.

In an evening of July
Souls are lit by fireflies.
Time alone will make them wise.

September 2015

Author's Note: This work is a tribute to "Alice's Poem" by Lewis Carroll. I followed the rhythm of Carroll's words, borrowed the last line of each stanza and reversed their order, transforming them into the first line of each of my own stanzas. —A.B. Flynn

THIS MEANS WAR

Moments.

Unable to be recounted.

And yet I do.

Like a golden film of yesteryear it plays before me.

The time when your eyes were so close

To mine

That our souls kissed

And in that instant

I became a sunrise.

Two hands.

Accidental.

Nothing that means anything.

And yet it is all.

When such things transpire who can fight the fates?

It is useless,

But still I strive.

I surrender,

But I will not be beaten.

There is more than just eternal happiness.

November 2015

WORDS WRITTEN IN A COFFEE SHOP
A YEAR AND A MONTH AGO

There is a dragon fighting a mother-of-pearl unicorn outside my bedroom window. The trees groan, trying to bear the weight of the brawl. The leaves flutter to the ground, quickly forgotten consequences of the war above.

The dragon breathes fire, its claws silver with unicorn blood, yet its foe is unharmed. The unicorn horn glistens like the trophy of a battle already won. I cannot choose sides for that would be to make an enemy of myself. I am both adversaries, and it is myself who wars.

Reason, like a dragon of fury, quick to draw blood and destroy, is after the unicorn of my dreams, a thing of beauty that is not meant for battle. But it is armed with a weapon sharper than glass, able to pierce the heart of logic at the slightest provocation.

They battle today, and they will battle tomorrow. And all I can do is watch, and mourn, and celebrate both the victor and the vanquished. I know that neither will ever win, but that they will war, on and on, until the creases around my mouth have deepened, and the wrinkles hide my eyes, and I am crowned with immortality.

It is a losing battle, and yet I am the victor.

January 2016

THE ANGEL ON MY DOORSTEP

There is an angel on my doorstep
Bare feet in newly fallen snow
Eyes, grey like storm clouds, dark rimmed with sleeplessness.
Hands warm despite their paleness
Holding my heart
And I can hear the sounds of violins.

My daily visitor
Brief but regular
Until I could not imagine each morning without her.
There is a comfort in sameness, even if it is imagined.
Celestial beings can touch the souls of mortals
But they must pay the highest price.

Sudden vacancy.
Silence
As if the love of humankind was too much.
I did not mean to drive her away.
If she only knew the emptiness
Without the burning of her fingertips.

I am aged.

This is the last of my mornings.

The angel's empty footprints are on my doorstep

Perfect in the mound of white.

The human heart beats warmer one final time.

The violins start to play.

January 2016

Words
that fly from fingertips
so easily sent into the world
without fear of regret
until I do

Words
held captive in the silence of fear
lips sealed shut
the moment passes
the deepest longing denied

Words
that could break the spell
if only permitted
and release my pounding heart from prison
just by the utterance

Why must one rise on one's own two feet in order to stand?

Cannot I just say the words and be set free?

December 2016

2017

The days are fresh ahead
like newly fallen snow before the world has awakened to its presence.

My feet are weary from the dance,
yet they continue onward,
tempted by the promise of joy and success to come.

The old lies behind me already gathering dust.
It drifts across the lips of boys I did not kiss,
the words I was supposed to say already forgotten,
never to be recounted.

Even now I feel the weight of the unvoiced,
the burden of an unexplored future,
even as I let the load of what is past fall from my shoulders and step,
unhindered,
across the threshold of time.

The year is new.

My heart still sings.

I will walk on.

January 2017

CANDOR

The day hurts.
The waking. The working.
Sometimes
Even the time to close our eyes.
It is too much to be borne.

There is something more.
Enough to survive.
Enough
To make the burden bearable.
Maybe even to walk free.

February 2017

BRAVE ENOUGH

I have the courage to fight the war,
and I know the words to call the butterflies.

I've got stamina, and I will follow the golden tail of a meteor
Until it plummets into the sea.
I can hold the breath in my lungs until I reach the ocean floor.

My words are smooth.
I have reasoned with the mermaids,
the silver creatures who drown the souls of men
and leave their bodies to rise again to the surface.

My heart is strong
but soft enough to sense the murmuring of the white stags,
and my feet are swift to follow.

The woods no longer call me the way they used to,
and the mountains have grown silent.
My footsteps no longer echo,
and my shadow has returned to its home.

My foes surround me,
relentless,
waiting to claim my being.

All is silence.
Much has been lost.

Why must there always be dragons?

I am brave enough.

February 2017

A PLEA

I am lacking
> My heart is empty
> Hollow
> Echoing
> Like a tomb that has given up its dead.

Must I stay
> Wrists bound
> Lips silent
> Heart still?
> I need a breath of hope to fill my lungs.

How can I be released when I do not believe?
> I do believe.
> Help my unbelief.

March 2017

THE DETOUR

I walked among the tombs tonight,
Just for a change, to wend my way,
And on each grave shone fairy lights
Lit from the sunbeams of the day.

I chose a path not often walked
To test my surety of step,
And hide my face from human talk
And cloak the human tears I wept.

The night wind called my name aloud;
Absent voices cried a warning.
I was alone amidst the crowd,
My heart within a burial shroud.
Yet purpose clear, and spirit proud,
I pressed onward towards the morning.

March 2017

WAKE ME

My heart beats
>Sudden in the silence
>While the world pounds around me
>Endless noise, never pausing to catch breath
>My skin is hot with the fire of living
>But my heart
>My heart
>Cold
>Cold and numb

I need to feel more than life burning all around me
>And I need to hear more than the din above the quiet
>And then maybe the ice will melt at last

It is too much to hope

April 2017

'TIS BETTER

They say 'tis better to have loved and lost
    Than never to have loved at all

But I think that he who wrote those words never truly heard the cry
of love

He could not have felt the burn of passion
The cruel twist of fate
The adoration

The sudden ceasing of the heart to beat
    After it finally breaks

May 2017

WHEN YOU LET SOMEONE GO

I tried to save the day,

To swoop in like a mighty warrior,

And defeat the foes who were breaking down your door.

But my armor was not strong enough for two,

And if I gave it to you then I would l be left unprotected.

Perhaps it is most honorable to sacrifice one's self,

But I was too afraid.

My words were big, but my soul was not as calloused.

I had the courage to stand on my feet

And possibly the gumption to survive,

But I couldn't fight your battles,

And I couldn't protect your heart.

I can't be your hero.

You must save yourself.

May 2017

THERE IS STILL HOPE

Too long have I hidden from the light:
Wearied of the world and afraid to reveal the truth of myself.
My soul grew darker in the shadows until it fell asleep
And it did not want to waken.

Let my heart be unshackled.
Let me walk the pathways of the living with a sure step.
Let the light shine upon my upturned face once more.
There is still hope.

May 2017

I AM THE GIRL WITH EMPTY HANDS

I will let go of my love.
I do not need it to survive.
It does my spirit mortal harm
And turns my soul into a desert.

I will not suffer anymore
Nor mourn the loss of what has never been.
The actualization of joy is a rare thing
And standing in the shadows the more certain fate.

I am happy for you, my friend.
It is my duty, but I am sincere.
The world will fall at your feet like the woman you love,
And I will watch, the girl with the empty hands.

It has been thus all along,
And it is easy to hide when one is always alone.
But even though I did not build a boat
Somehow I am left standing after the flood tide.

I will still breathe.
The heart within me will beat again.
Even the darkest hour must end at last,
And already I have lived to tell the tale.

I will let life come at me once more
And open wide my arms to receive it.
And even now I will find each small happiness
While I wait awhile in this useless passion.

June 2017

I WALK THE STREETS OF OUR TINY CITY

I walk the streets of our tiny city
The lights shining from every window
Welcoming the stranger
The doors locked
Barring me from pleasure
My footsteps my only companion
My hand empty where yours should be

You are locked behind a window
Wrapped inside the warmth
While my breath freezes on the air
And the wind chills my heart until the very beat slows

I will not survive the night

December 2017

MY SECRET BURDEN

The heaviness is unseen
But nonetheless is real
Truly, the burden hurts the most when no one spies it
Or acknowledges the weight of pain

And so I carry the burden alone
And hold up a smiling face
And envy the grief of my fellow man
Who parades his burden in the darkness and the light

One cannot help what one does not feel
Any more than one can stop the loving

February 2018

THE DETOUR — PART II

How can the sickness be the cure,
And torment soften every pain,
And still my heart feel vast and pure
While lying trapped within these chains?

How can I be the most myself
While shrouded still my face remains,
And find a freedom in the stealth
And fractured bliss within these chains?

I know the end will come in time.
I'll lose the heaven I have gained.
And yet I don't regret the crime.
This song is sweeter in the rhyme.
Athena yet remains divine,
And stronger than these blessed chains.

April 2018

MY SISTERS AND I

We are stronger
With our freckled eyes and the crease between our brows
And our jawlines set in determination

We walk sure
And the heads turn
And sometimes we even smile at the crowds
Yet they don't glimpse our shattered souls

We look ahead
And remember every moment
Every feeling
And every footstep is more resolute

We have survived
And someday maybe we will even prosper
We are lionhearted
My sisters and I

July 2018

A HAIKU

There are many tears
Perhaps I will drink coffee
Drown them completely

July 2018

FREE AGAIN

You tried to shackle me
Caught my wrists with your words and whispered your lies until my spirit broke

But I am free again

I can walk in the light
And I am not afraid to show the scars on my soul

I am my own once more

September 2018

STAGES OF GRIEF
OUT OF ORDER

Remember the day we first met
And all of the oxygen left the room?

—

Why does this feel like destiny
When it was never more than doomed?

—

Is that your breath or mine?
I cannot tell who I am
Where I end and you begin

—

Would this have happened if it weren't for that one night?
Was I just too weak to resist?
Or was this meant to be all along?

—

And I was left crying
But of course you didn't see the tears
That luxury is yours

—

Won't you stay a little bit longer
And pretend to hold my hand again

Even though we both know it means nothing?

—

This is my greatest challenge
My endless pain
I deserve relief

—

And now at last I know
What I am truly made of

—

I can't stay this way forever
Because I can't spend my life in suffering
Do I run away
Or fight the demons?
I can overcome
I believe

—

And this is the last time
You'll ever see me like this
I swear it

—

If I loved you for all eternity
Would you hold it against me?

—

I am no longer the person I thought I was
But I am braver
And more terrible

—

And still somehow there are stars in my eyes
Even though they all said I would be broken
I see more brilliantly now
Because I was blinded by you

—

If I had my way
I would breathe you in and out
Each day of my life

—

I am not the kind of woman they will celebrate or praise
But I can still tell stories
And paint pictures
And move in ways that make a human feel
So perhaps my purpose has not been lost
Even in the midst of this beautiful tragedy

—

If I can conquer this
I must be the strongest of them all

2018-2019

CAGED

I am pretty
Like a bird
Sitting in my golden cage

My master loves me
Admires my beauty
And the sweetness of my voice
But still I am a prisoner
This gold is still a cage

The door is open and I am able to fly
I could do so at any moment

But I wish to be coaxed to stay
I wish to be fed and petted
My master enraptured in the glory of my song

It's up to him

December 2018

CONSUMED

I do not fall easily
Or often
But when I do fall
It is hard
Unstoppable
Like a waterfall that spills over all my edges and drowns me
And I love with a fury that is impossible to stay, even for a moment

I am
Consumed

February 2019

THE SILENCE AND THE NOISE

When I hear my name on your lips
The earth is suddenly hushed
Spiritual stillness
The breath between us loud with purpose
And all I want is to be wrapped in your arms
To have the silence
And the noise
And the sound of my name
Be all that there is
Other than you

April 2019

HAIKU II

Your love is alive
Breath of fire on my body
Stillness in my soul

May 2019

I WATCH MY LADY FROM AFAR

I watch my lady from afar

The sunlight shamed by the scarlet of her tresses.

Her willowed figure—like a creature from another world.

When she turns, her eyes meet mine

And become a rainbow.

There is nothing more beautiful in the world.

She is my lady until eternity begins

May 2019

OPHELIA

And I loved him

More than I thought was possible.

More than anything I had ever loved and perhaps will love again.

That is the great tragedy of my life.

June 2019

THE QUEEN OF HEARTS

I am his queen

Right hand at his banquet seat.

From whence time began

It was our destiny.

Perhaps it was wrong

But I worshipped at his feet.

What else am I to do?

He is my king of hearts.

August 2019

THE DARK LORD SONNETS

I

How shall I speak to thee of my dark lord
And how he captured all my heart and soul?
The way he took my strength without a word
But left me always wanting, never whole?
He stole my body with his kisses sweet.
My arms will always feel the empty ache.
Yet worries fade within the ardor's heat
As he forswears all fortunes and all fates.
And when I went to turn away at last
He begged me sweetly with a final plea.
But all my heart went cold and I ran fast
And crushed his spirit as I turned to flee.
How could I leave the one who gave me breath
And force our love to face a living death?

II

How shall I speak to thee of my dark lord
And how he calmed my fears with gentle touch?
He ever was the one that I adored
Until the loving almost was too much.
His eyes were fathoms where I wished to drown,
His hair upon his brow of strength and grace,
And like a prince he seemed to wear a crown,
And faithfulness was written on his face.
His hands caressed my body, skin on skin,
His arms enfolded mine as if to shield
And free me from my doubting heart within.
One kiss from his soft lips, and I would yield.
And, day by day, I lived and loved my friend
As in a dream that seemed to never end.

III

How shall I speak to thee of my dark lord?
I've counted every moment since we met.
Each passioned day is one I still record,
And if I tried, no second I'd forget.
The way he trapped me in his loving arms
And broke my heart between his gentle hands,
Until my soul cried out in deep alarm
E'en as I let my body love the man.
Each day that passed brought with it painful fears
That all this beauty might indeed have end.
And time, before the passing of the year,
Would not just steal my lover, but my friend.
But still he does not heed the words I say,
And let me be the one that got away.

IV

How shall I speak to thee of my dark lord?
And how I spent each day his wrongful wife.
He vanquished all my strength with just a word,
Yet swore he'd guard me with his very life.
I try to paint him in my mind a saint
Despite this mortal crime to love him so,
But in my heart I know I'll bear the taint
Long after he has gone and let me go.
I must away and let the madness die
And find the peace this god destroyed in me.
My heart is cold; no tears left in my eyes.
His empty words at last force me flee.
My sin has taken love and made it cursed.
I plead, but he will never choose me first.

June 2018 - July 2019

THIS IS NOT THE END

Once it was always summer
And the sun never ceased to shine upon my upturned face
Even when it rained
And doused your hair
Which fell across your eyes, deep brown like the fresh earth.

The days ran in a circle of joy
And the forest echoed with the laughter of wood sprites.
We were children then
And we chased the light
As it fell like stardust through the spaces between the trees.

We were innocent
And nothing that was said or done could ever taint us.
My dreams were higher than the clouds
And each one attainable
As certain as the fact that you knew you'd find true love.

There's a photograph of us
Back before my dreams had died and your heart was broken.
Your face was close to mine
Our hands were clasped tight
And each moment spent together was as natural as breathing.

I thought I was the future
And that my hands would shake the very fibers of this world.
You thought that I was perfect
And that the signs were in your favor.
The time and place would come when all in love was right.

That was all so very long ago
Before the rungs of the ladder collapsed beneath my feet.
You tried to save me
And offer an escape
But I needed time and space to learn to fight the world on my own.

I wasted my best years
Chasing the straying sunbeams that slipped through my fingers
And left me wanting
My hands still empty.
The glittering renown I thought would find me proved elusive.

You suffered alone.
The years took the joy and triumph from your footsteps.
The brown eyes lost their mirth.
Stranded on an island of your building
You fled from the elements and the pain inside your own being.

There were no more words:
No reason to share the secrets of our hearts.
I took my own counsel
Carried my own soul
Until the weight of it brought me to the earth, beaten in the end.

I saw you again.
Your hair across your forehead like the child I once knew.
But delight was gone
Hope and desire faded
Resignation painted across the visage that had been my closest friend.

No more.

Take my hand.
The woods we used to roam are still alive and breathing.
The sunlit showers fall just the same
And there is joy yet to be found.
The light continues to call us, and the earth has room for love and
dreams.

We are children still.

July 2017

Acknowledgements

Thank you to all the boys I loved and lost—the pain helped me grow into a poet. To Alyssa, Mindy, and Ramon, for being there for me through the hard years. Forever grateful to you, Mum, for always being my number-one cheerleader.

Aunt Cari—Carilyn Flynn—thank you for being one of my earliest poetry influences. You introduced me to so much great literature and have supported me on every step of my life and literary journey. It is an honor to now have you as my editor!

Thank you to Wendy Flynn and Nicole Eckerson for reading this collection and providing feedback, and to Ani Gjika for being a poetic inspiration and answering all my publishing questions!

So much gratitude to you, Ryan, for lighting up my life with your kisses and constant antics. I love you.

About the Author

Amanda Beth Flynn was born and raised in Massachusetts and considers New England the most beautiful place on earth. Her writing is inspired by her unconventional childhood—growing up as the oldest of eleven children—her favorite authors: J.M. Barrie, L.M. Montgomery, L.M. Alcott, C.S. Lewis, Elizabeth George Speare, Agatha Christie, and Rosemary Sutcliffe, and her connection to nature.

Amanda has been writing poems and stories since she first put pen to paper and dreaming big dreams of publishing her work for decades. *The Poems of Lucy Snowe* is her first self-published offering.

In addition to writing, Amanda's hobbies include spending time in nature, psychology *and* astrology, crochet, and all things creative. She lives with her partner, Ryan, and their dogs, Koopa and Navi, in a small town and watches reruns of *Gilmore Girls* all year-round.

If you enjoy her writing, please visit Amanda's website at
amandabethflynn.com
She can also be found on Instagram and TikTok @amandabethflynn

www.ingramcontent.com/pod-product-compliance
Lightning Source LLC
Chambersburg PA
CBHW030238150726
47988CB00021B/3155